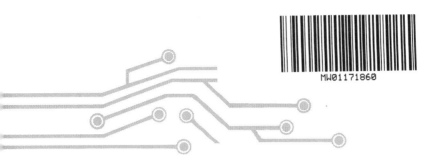

WINNING
FROM MY LOSSES

By Kelle Daniels

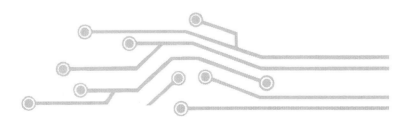

To my beloved daughter,

I give all praise, glory, and honor to God for the journey He has brought you through. You've kept the faith, even in the most difficult times, and your perseverance has led you to this incredible milestone—your first book publication. It's a joy and a blessing to witness you blossom into the woman I prayed and believed God for.

From the many seeds sown into your life, and even the losses you've endured, God has used it all to bring about victory. Your dedication, resilience, and faithfulness have borne fruit, and I couldn't be prouder of you. This is only the beginning of what He has in store. Keep shining, keep walking in purpose, and keep trusting His plan.

With all my love,
Mrs. Wanda F. Norris Daniels
(The late Dr. Dempsey Daniels)

Dear Visionary Builder,

First, let me say how honored I am that you've chosen to open this book. Win From My Losses isn't just a collection of strategies or anecdotes—it's a personal exchange of lessons, hard-earned through my own experiences. I've walked the path of building, failing, and rebuilding, and I'm sharing this with you to provide insights, strategies, and solace as you embark on your own journey.

The process of building anything—a business, a dream, or a legacy—is not without its challenges. Building a business can be exciting and rewarding. However, you will encounter disappointments, setbacks, and moments of doubt. These are not signs of failure but necessary elements of growth. Through this book, I aim to equip you with the tools to navigate these challenges, to show you that every setback has a lesson embedded in it, and that with the right perspective and preparation, you can emerge stronger.

I've poured my story into these pages, not to focus on my losses but to illuminate how they've shaped my wins. My hope is that by sharing my failures—every misstep, every moment of grief, and every hard-won lesson—you can sidestep some of the obstacles I faced or approach them with greater readiness.

Remember, your journey will have its own unique

variables, and no two paths are the same. Yet the principles of building—vision, resilience, adaptability, and persistence— remain universal. Through this book, I want to remind you that while the process is challenging, it is also deeply rewarding. Each brick you lay in your journey is a testament to your courage and determination.

This book is more than a guide; it's a partnership. My losses are your opportunities to win. I encourage you to approach each chapter with curiosity and openness, applying what resonates and discarding what doesn't. As you read, know that you are not alone in this journey—I'm here, rooting for you, and so are countless others who have walked the path of visionaries and builders.

Thank you for trusting me to be part of your journey.

Let's build something extraordinary together.

Table Of Content

Chapter 1
Introduction: Building in Every Season

In this chapter you will learn starting a business is exciting but also daunting. Growth comes in waves, and success demands adaptability. This chapter provides actionable advice for navigating:

- Seasons of growth when demand surges.
- Lean times when capital is tight.
- Emotional challenges that threaten your resilience.

You'll learn to stay the course, adapt to change, and cultivate a mindset that sustains both you and your business.

Building a business is not a linear journey; it's an evolving process marked by distinct seasons, each with its own challenges and opportunities. During periods of growth, the temptation may be to ride the wave and overextend resources to meet increasing demand. However, sustainable growth comes from scaling wisely streamlining operations, automating processes, and ensuring your team is prepared for expansion. Focus on maintaining quality and managing customer expectations, as these are the cornerstones of long-term success.

In lean times, financial prudence is critical. Use this season to evaluate what's working and trim unnecessary expenses. This is also the time to focus on relationships... reconnect with past clients, nurture your network, and explore low-cost marketing strategies that emphasize your brand's value and story. Lean periods are opportunities to refine your business model, enhance efficiency, and build resilience.

The emotional challenges of entrepreneurship are perhaps the least discussed but most critical to address. Feelings of isolation, self-doubt, or burnout are common, especially when your business isn't performing as expected. This is where having strong systems, mentors, or a coach can provide perspective and support. Cultivate habits that sustain you whether it's regular exercise, mindfulness practices, or connecting with other business owners who understand your journey.

Adaptability is the skill that ties all these elements together. Recognizing that seasons of growth, stagnation, and retraction are natural allows you to approach each phase with a clear, strategic mindset. Success isn't about avoiding difficulties—it's about learning to navigate them with confidence and intention. My goal is to arm you with the insights, tools, and strategies to ensure you're not only building a business but building one that lasts.

Chapter 2
Starting Smart: Building a Business with Limited Capital

According to the SBA*, lack of capital is the second most common reason small businesses fail. Headd, B. (2018, May). **Small business facts: Why do businesses close? U.S. Small Business Administration, Office of Advocacy**. *Retrieved from https://advocacy.sba.gov.*

Starting a business with limited capital is a common challenge, yet it can also be an opportunity to build a lean, efficient, and creative foundation. According to the U.S. Small Business Administration, lack of capital is the second most common reason small businesses fail, yet many successful entrepreneurs started with minimal resources by making strategic choices and maximizing what they had.

Building a Business with Limited Capital: Practical Strategies for Success

Here's how you can do the same, with actionable methods for application:

Low-Cost Strategies

Spend wisely on essentials like professional branding and a functional website. These are long-term investments in your credibility.

Low-Cost Strategies for Starting and Building a Business

Spending wisely on essentials like professional branding and a functional website is crucial when starting out. These aren't just expenses—they're long-term investments in your credibility and the foundation for attracting customers. As a business owner, prioritizing what truly matters over superficial extras can make the difference between struggling and thriving.

I started all my business endeavors with little to no upfront capital. One business was entirely funded out of my personal savings, which were meant to sustain my living expenses. Another was 30% funded by those who believed in my vision, while the remainder came directly from my pocket.

The pressure to meet traditional standards, without fully respecting my unique circumstances, led to mental fatigue and emotional strain. I often felt the weight of trying to appear as though I had everything figured out when in reality, I needed creative solutions and strategic partnerships.

The grief of those missteps and the losses I endured far outweighed the wins numerically. But through those experiences, I learned valuable lessons: respecting my starting point, finding innovative ways to plan, and building connections that could support my vision were just as important as hard work. I've since grown to see that wins don't always come from doing things the way others do—they come from staying true to your path and making thoughtful, strategic decisions based on where you are.

To those starting out, I encourage you to invest where it truly counts. Focus on functionality and growth and remember that your journey doesn't have to look like anyone else's. Creativity and resourcefulness are your greatest allies, and every thoughtful step you take builds a foundation for lasting success.

Grassroots Marketing

The Power of Connections: Grassroots marketing is about creating meaningful connections within your community. Attending local events, joining industry meetups, or participating in community initiatives where potential clients or collaborators gather. This builds trust and credibility without significant expense.

How to Apply:

i. Identify community events, trade shows, or networking groups relevant to your industry. By engaging and connecting in this way, you open the door to building relationships that might not have been possible otherwise. Putting a face to a name and fostering person-to-person interactions builds trust and strengthens rapport. These connections create opportunities for deeper collaboration and lasting partnerships.

ii. Prepare an elevator pitch about your business and bring simple but professional marketing materials like business cards or brochures. An **elevator pitch** is a short, clear, and compelling description of your business or idea that you can deliver in the time it takes to ride an elevator—usually 30 seconds to a minute.

iii. It's important because it helps you quickly communicate the value of your business to potential clients, investors, or partners. A great elevator pitch grabs attention, makes a strong first impression, and opens the door to more meaningful conversations about your business.

iv. Follow up with new connections on social media or via email, fostering relationships that can lead to referrals and collaborations.

Networking effectively starts with a clear purpose. Before connecting with others, know what you want to achieve, whether it's finding clients, partners, or mentors. Prepare a short introduction about who you are, what you do, and how you add value to make a strong impression. Focus on attending events or groups that align with your business goals and take the time to ask questions and listen. Showing genuine interest builds trust and leaves a lasting positive impression. Afterward, follow up with a thank-you message to maintain the connection.

Mentally preparing for networking requires shifting your mindset from seeking what you can gain to thinking about how you can add value to others. Remind yourself that everyone is there for similar reasons, and your unique perspective has something to offer. Visualize success by imagining productive conversations and meaningful connections. Release the pressure of needing to "perform" perfectly and instead focus on building genuine relationships. Confidence comes from preparation, so trust your value, stay curious, and let your authenticity lead the way.

Motivational Truth: Turning Losses into Wins

For me, networking didn't come naturally. I used to watch individuals who carried themselves in ways I admired, and I began to model their methods. At first, I didn't have my own approach, but I was determined to learn. I turned to YouTube, researching topics like "how to network" and whether someone with a not-so-outgoing personality could succeed in building connections. I dove deep into understanding how to develop a mindset that aligned with my goals, and slowly, things started to shift.

What I didn't expect was the personal journey it would take me on. I discovered that my struggles weren't just about learning new techniques—they were about healing old wounds. Rejection, fear of "no," and the weight of past disappointments had created a warped perspective that held me back. It wasn't just networking that felt dreadful; it was the vulnerability required to put myself out there. I realized those fears weren't just blocking my professional growth—they were infringing on my ability to market my business in ways that extended beyond the safety of my keyboard.

Through intentional effort and a willingness to confront those fears, I began to unlock what was once so intimidating. Networking became less about perfection and more about connection. The same thing that once felt like a barrier became a tool for growth and empowerment. My losses taught me that fear doesn't have to win, and rejection is not the end—it's a step closer to clarity and resilience.

To anyone struggling with the same fears, know this:

growth requires courage, but courage grows with each step you take. Learn, adapt, and let go of the fear of failure. What's on the other side of those challenges is more than success; it's freedom from the limits you once believed you couldn't overcome. If I can win from my losses, so can you.

Your Digital Storefront: Free tools to showcase your work, share your story, and connect with customers. Authenticity and consistency are key—engage your audience with content that reflects your values and highlights your expertise.

Here are five examples of **Your Digital Storefront** to showcase your business online:

1. **Social Media Pages:** Platforms like Instagram, Facebook, and LinkedIn allow you to showcase your offerings, engage with your audience, and build brand awareness.

2. **E-commerce Platforms:** Online marketplaces such as Shopify, Etsy, or Amazon where customers can browse and purchase your products.

3. **Google My Business Profile:** A free tool to manage how your business appears on Google Search and Maps, making it easier for local customers to find you.

4. **Online Portfolios or Catalogs:** Platforms like

Behance or Issuu to display your work or product offerings in a professional and visually appealing way.

How to Apply:

i.   Create a content calendar to post consistently (e.g., 3–5 times a week). Use a mix of posts, including behind-the-scenes updates, testimonials, tips, and promotions.

ii. Engage with your audience by responding to comments and messages promptly. Use polls, questions, and live videos to increase interaction.

iii. Track performance using platform analytics to see what resonates most with your audience and adjust your strategy accordingly.

Trading Skills for Growth: Bartering allows you to exchange your skills for the resources you need without spending money. For instance, if you're a web designer, you can trade your expertise with a photographer for high-quality product photos or with a copywriter for compelling website content.

How to Apply:

i.   Make a list of your skills and the resources or services you need.

ii. Network within your industry or community to find professionals whose skills complement your needs.

iii. Propose a barter agreement that outlines the scope of work for both parties, ensuring clear expectations and timelines.

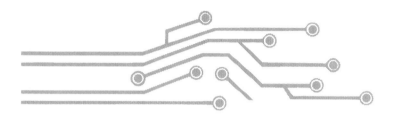

Chapter 3
The Value of Systems: Laying the Foundation for Longevity

Why Systems Matter:

Without systems, businesses fail to scale. Systems reduce stress, improve consistency, and save time. Think of systems as the infrastructure that allows your business to grow smoothly. **My Lessons Learned from Operating Without Systems and Strategy**

For the first four years of my business, I operated without systems or strategic insight, relying solely on social media to drive website traffic. Despite my efforts, I only achieved a 30% increase in website views—a sobering reflection of my lack of knowledge and direction. My ignorance of key tools like SEO tracking and analytics hindered my ability to connect with my target market effectively.

I failed to take advantage of the free insights provided by social media platforms, such as understanding what content resonated most with my audience. Instead of analyzing data to refine my approach, I kept posting blindly, hoping for results. My lack of diligence in studying business trends further compounded the problem, leaving me disconnected from what my audience truly wanted and how the market was evolving.

I failed to take advantage of the free insights provided by social media platforms, such as understanding what content resonated most with my audience. Instead of analyzing data to refine my approach, I kept posting blindly, hoping for results. My lack of diligence in studying business trends further compounded the problem, leaving me disconnected from what my audience truly wanted and how the market was evolving.

I also underestimated the power of automation to save time and improve productivity. Expecting success while ignoring tools that could streamline my processes was a costly mistake. My inefficiency and reliance on outdated methods led to frustration and missed opportunities.

This experience taught me a valuable lesson: growth requires intentionality. Implementing systems, understanding analytics, and prioritizing automation are non-negotiable for scaling a business effectively. Moving forward, I've committed to leveraging these tools and strategies to ensure my business operates with focus, efficiency, and purpose.

Key Systems to Implement:

- **Templates:** Create reusable templates for contracts, proposals, and communications. Creating reusable templates for contracts, proposals, and communications saves time, ensures consistency, and maintains a professional image. They streamline repetitive tasks, reduce errors, and allow you to focus on higher-value activities, improving efficiency and client experience.

Invest Where It Matters

Even with limited capital, some investments are non-negotiable for building credibility and professionalism. Prioritize spending on:

- **A Functional Website**: In today's digital age, a website is often your first impression. Invest in a simple but well-designed site that showcases your offerings, testimonials, and contact information. A **functional website** is critical because it serves as your business's digital storefront and often makes the first impression on potential customers. A well-designed, easy-to-navigate site showcases your offerings, builds credibility, and provides essential information like testimonials and contact details, making it easier for customers to trust and engage with your business.

The Power of Systems and Strategic Growth: Lessons from My Journey

Often times, we want our immediate circle to become our primary clients, but in my experience, true growth comes from reaching beyond familiar faces. The people who have supported my business the most were often strangers I never would have met had I not marketed strategically. As a graduate of a marketplace institute where media development was ingrained, I learned that entering the marketplace with a solid foundation gives your business or vision a significant edge. It positions you to reach audiences far beyond your immediate network and increases the likelihood of your success.

But the journey has not been without challenges. In the early stages of my business, I wore every hat—visionary, administrator, salesperson, closer, bookkeeper, and even maintenance system. It was overwhelming. There were days when my business wasn't marketed because I was mentally and emotionally drained. I lacked systems to keep operations running smoothly, and it showed. I remember times when I over-booked appointments because I was trying to juggle word-of-mouth referrals, DMs, and an underutilized booking site. My hunger for sales led to chaos, and I wasn't managing my processes well.

Then came the harder moments—times when I wasn't physically well, and my business went down with me, financially included. The pressure of knowing that nothing could run without me was crushing. I felt devastated, trapped under the weight of it all, and there were countless moments when I wanted to quit. My lack of systems wasn't just costing me money; it was costing me peace.

However, the story doesn't end there. Through those challenges, I discovered the blessing of wisdom and tools that transformed how I built and ran my business. I learned to slow down and embrace the building process rather than rushing for quick fixes. Implementing systems—automated scheduling, customer relationship management tools, and marketing strategies—allowed my business to grow with me. Instead of being weighed down, I began to experience freedom. These systems didn't just support my business; they supported me as a visionary.

With systems in place, I could focus on what mattered most—delivering value, nurturing relationships, and stepping into the marketplace with confidence. No longer was I throwing money at quick marketing ideas in desperation; I was making informed decisions that aligned with my vision and long-term goals.

The greatest lesson I've learned is this: a business built with intention and supported by the right tools becomes more than just a source of income. It becomes a reflection of your wisdom, creativity, and resilience. When you take the time to establish systems, you create a foundation that not only sustains your business but also sustains you as its leader. Today, I'm grateful for the challenges because they taught me how to build a business that works for me—not one that drains me.

For every visionary out there, know this: the tools and strategies you invest in now will become the lifeline of your business tomorrow. Build with intention, embrace systems, and allow your vision to flourish beyond what you could ever imagine. The marketplace is waiting, and you are more than capable of thriving in it.

Applying These Principles for Success
Focus on High-Impact Activities

Allocate your time and resources to activities that directly generate leads or build trust. For instance, if most of your clients come from social media, focus on improving your content and engagement strategy in that area.

Measure and Optimize

Track the effectiveness of your efforts using free tools like Google Analytics for your website or insights provided by social media platforms. Use this data to refine your approach, doubling down on what works and eliminating what doesn't.

Why Tracking and Optimization Are Effective

Sharing my earnings and allowing tools like Domain. com to evaluate my performance globally was a humbling yet eye-opening experience. It forced me to confront areas where my business wasn't meeting its potential. For example, seeing how far my revenue was from the industry average helped me understand the critical gaps in my operations and marketing efforts. These insights weren't just numbers—they were roadmaps to better decision-making.

Free tools like Google Analytics and social media insights became essential in turning my business around. Instead of guessing what content would work, I saw exactly what resonated with my audience and what fell flat. By focusing on the data, I shifted my efforts to strategies that produced tangible results, like posting more of the content that generated high engagement and cutting out the types that didn't.

Optimization wasn't just about improving numbers— it was about regaining control. Tracking my efforts allowed me to understand my audience better, streamline my operations, and ensure that my energy and resources were being spent where they mattered most. Seeing those numbers transformed my approach from reactive to proactive, saving time, money, and frustration while positioning my business for sustainable growth.

Leverage Your Network

Tap into existing relationships to spread the word about your business. Reach out to friends, family, and past colleagues to share your services. Referrals from trusted connections are often the fastest way to secure your first few clients.

The Power of Tapping Into Existing Relationships.

When I first heard the advice to tap into my existing relationships to spread the word about my business, I hesitated. As a visionary, I wasn't naturally drawn to large groups or crowds. Being a visionary doesn't necessarily mean you have a big personality or thrive in social settings—it often means you're focused on building, creating, and refining your vision. Even as someone comfortable speaking, the idea of intentionally reaching out, showing up, and introducing myself felt daunting.

But I quickly realized that my comfort zone was also my limitation. As much as I loved working quietly in my own space, that approach meant I was the only one who truly understood or appreciated my business. Without putting myself in the right spaces and engaging in the right conversations, I risked becoming my only customer. Being a great visionary and builder doesn't matter if no one knows you exist or understands how you can help them.

The turning point for me was recognizing that referrals and word-of-mouth connections are incredibly powerful, especially when they come from trusted sources. Friends, family, and colleagues already had networks of people who might need my services, but they couldn't advocate for me if they didn't fully know what I offered or who I was trying to reach. By stepping into rooms that I wouldn't normally frequent and being intentional about sharing my story, I created opportunities I never would have found otherwise.

What I learned is that being intentional about connecting with others is just as important as the work you do behind the scenes. The right spaces and conversations are a necessity for making an impact. By tapping into existing relationships and extending beyond them with purpose, I began to see how much value others could add to my journey—and how much value I could provide in return. The discomfort was temporary, but the rewards have been lasting.

Starting with limited capital is not a limitation but an opportunity to unlock your creativity, resourcefulness, and strategic thinking. By focusing on impactful strategies like grassroots marketing, digital tools, and meaningful partnerships, you can build a strong foundation without overextending your resources.

Thoughtful investments in the right areas will allow your business to grow steadily and sustainably, proving that success is achievable no matter where you start.

Stay focused, stay resilient, and watch your vision thrive!

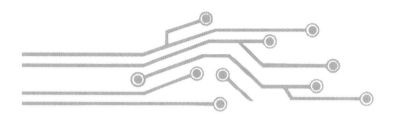

Chapter 4
Enduring Emotional and Financial Lows

"Over 50% of small businesses fail within five years. Many owners cite emotional burnout as a contributing factor." **Headd, B.** *(2018, May).* **Small business facts: Why do businesses close?** U.S. Small Business Administration, Office of Advocacy. Retrieved from *https://advocacy.sba.gov*

Strategies to Cope:
- **Set Realistic Expectations:** Understand that growth takes time. Overnight success is a myth.
- **Build a Support Network:** Join business owner groups or mentorship programs to share experiences and gain perspective.
- **Prioritize Mental Health:** Regular exercise, mindfulness,

and time with loved ones can keep you grounded.

The Value of Systems: Laying the Foundation for Longevity

For any business to thrive and scale, implementing effective systems is not optional—it's essential. Systems streamline operations, minimize errors, and allow solopreneurs to focus on high-impact tasks instead of being bogged down by repetitive or administrative work. Research shows that 82% of businesses fail due to cash flow problems, inefficiencies, or burnout, many of which can be mitigated with proper systems. Beyond operational efficiency, systems also enhance professionalism, improve customer satisfaction, and help solopreneurs build a business that operates consistently, even under pressure.

Why Systems Matter?
Scalability and Efficiency

Without systems, a business can only grow to the capacity of the owner's time and energy—a finite resource. Systems provide the framework to scale by delegating tasks to tools or teams and ensuring processes are repeatable. *Forbes. (n.d.). CRM tools and business growth. Retrieved from https:// www.forbes.com*

Practical Example: A business with a CRM tool like HubSpot can manage 50 leads with the same effort as 5 leads by automating follow-ups, reminders, and data tracking.

Why Systems Matter: Scalability and Efficiency

Without systems, a business is limited to the capacity of the owner's time and energy, which are finite resources. Systems provide the structure to scale, enabling tasks to be delegated to tools or teams and ensuring processes are repeatable. This frees the business owner from being the bottleneck and allows growth without constant burnout.

My own journey taught me this lesson the hard way. My loss was not in lacking knowledge of the tools, but in allowing personal frustration and disappointment along with certain teachers to keep me separated from the very methods and practices I should have been applying. Instead of focusing on the tools themselves, I allowed my emotions to block my progress, delaying the establishment of systems that could have served me well.

Over time, humility and sensibility brought me to a place of clarity. I realized that what I've learned—despite the circumstances—was given to me to thrive and prosper. Systems aren't just about organization. They're about creating spaces for growth and peace, ensuring that my vision wasn't limited by my own capacity and supported by thoughtful, scalable processes.

Learning the Value of Prioritizing Systems Over Appearance

I've come to realize that implementing systems was not just helpful—it was essential. Looking back, I missed significant growth opportunities in the earlier stages of my business, even after witnessing their effectiveness in marketplace school. I saw how systems consistently drove sales from new customers and repeat business from existing clients. Yet, I neglected this crucial aspect, and as a result, I missed out on both revenue and valuable relationships.

The truth is, I sacrificed the wrong things. Instead of prioritizing functionality and scalability, I focused too much on appearances—how fancy things looked rather than how well they worked. This mindset slowed my growth and added unnecessary frustration.

Now, I understand that building effective systems should be a top priority. It's not about looking polished first; it's about creating a functional, revenue-generating foundation. Once the systems are in place and the business is thriving, you can invest in making things look fancy. Functionality drives growth, and growth creates the resources to refine your presentation. I'm committed to implementing this approach moving forward, and I already see the potential it brings for consistency and success.

Reducing Stress for Solopreneurs

Solopreneurs often juggle every aspect of their business—marketing, client relations, operations, and finance. Without systems, this juggling act can lead to overwhelm, mistakes, and eventual burnout.

How Systems Help: Automating routine tasks like invoicing or scheduling creates mental space, enabling the solopreneur to focus on strategic growth.

Statistical Insight: Businesses with automated workflows experience 15% higher productivity and 10% greater work-life balance for owners. *McKinsey & Company. (n.d.). The value of automated workflows in businesses. Retrieved from https:// www.mckinsey.com*

Enhancing Consistency: Systems create consistency in service delivery, which directly impacts customer trust and satisfaction. Consistent experiences encourage repeat business and strengthen your brand identity. .

Practical Example: Using templates for client communications ensures every customer interaction aligns with your brand tone, eliminating the variability that can occur with ad-hoc approaches.

Key Systems to Implement
Customer Relationship Management (CRM)

A CRM system tracks customer interactions, manages leads, and ensures no opportunity falls through the cracks. For solopreneurs, this means staying on top of follow-ups and nurturing leads efficiently.

How It Works: Tools like HubSpot or Zoho allow you to track the status of leads, schedule emails, and analyze customer trends—all in one place.

Impact: Studies show that businesses using CRM systems can boost sales by 29% and customer retention by 27%. (*Nucleus Research. (2014).* **CRM pays back $8.71 for every dollar spent.** *Retrieved from https://nucleusresearch.com)*

Automation Tools

Automation reduces the manual workload for repetitive tasks like invoicing, scheduling, and email follow-ups.

How It Works: Tools like Zapier connect apps and automate workflows, while tools like QuickBooks streamline invoicing.

Impact: Solopreneurs who automate routine tasks report feeling 30% less overwhelmed and can reallocate time to strategic initiatives. *Small Business Trends. (2021).* **Automation reduces workload and increases productivity in small businesses.** *Retrieved from https://smallbiztrends.com*

Templates

Templates standardize processes, saving time and ensuring consistency in your communications and contracts.

How It Works: Create reusable documents for proposals, contracts, and email responses to streamline repetitive tasks.

Impact: Templates can reduce drafting time by up to 80%, allowing solopreneurs to focus on their core services.

How Systems Challenge Growth and Boost Business Character
Promoting Strategic Thinking

Implementing systems forces solopreneurs to think critically about their processes, identify inefficiencies, and optimize workflows. This fosters a growth-oriented mindset and encourages continuous improvement.

Example: Setting up a CRM may initially feel daunting, but it requires analyzing your customer journey—this clarity often leads to insights that refine your business strategy.

Building Professionalism

Customers expect a polished and reliable experience. Systems create a sense of professionalism by ensuring that services are delivered consistently and efficiently.

Statistical Insight: 73% of customers cite consistency as a critical factor in brand loyalty. *PwC. (2018).* **Experience is everything: Here's how to get it right.** *Retrieved from https://www.pwc.com*

Practical Example: Automated follow-up emails ensure clients never feel forgotten, reflecting positively on your business.

Enabling Delegation

As a business grows, systems make it easier to delegate tasks to employees or freelancers without sacrificing quality or consistency. This is essential for scaling beyond what a single person can handle.

Impact: A documented process is 2.5 times more likely to be executed effectively when handed off to a team member. *Harvard Business Review. (2016).* **How to document and scale processes in growing businesses.** *Retrieved from https://hbr. org*

Alleviating Pressure on the Solopreneur

The pressure to manage every aspect of a business can lead to decision fatigue, errors, and burnout. Systems alleviate this by:

- **Streamlining Decisions:** Predefined workflows and templates eliminate the need to reinvent processes for every task.
- **Reducing Errors:** Automation and consistency reduce human error, particularly in administrative or repetitive tasks.
- **Creating Breathing Room:** By taking over mundane tasks, systems free up time for strategic planning, creative thinking, or even personal rejuvenation.

A Foundation for Longevity

Think of systems as the invisible scaffolding holding your business together. They may require an upfront investment of time and effort, but the returns are exponential. Systems allow you to build a business that runs smoothly, scales effortlessly, and projects reliability—an essential ingredient for long-term success. Whether you're just starting or preparing for growth, implementing the right systems is one of the smartest decisions you can make.

Enduring Emotional and Financial Lows: Building Resilience from the Inside Out

The journey of business ownership is as much an emotional endeavor as it is a financial and operational one. The statistic that over 50% of small businesses fail within five years is often framed as a financial challenge, but the emotional toll is equally significant. *Commerce Institute.(2024).* **What percentage of businesses fail each year?** (2024 data). *Retrieved from https://www.commerceinstitute.com/business-failure-rate/*

Many entrepreneurs have found themselves in a cycle of burnout, poor decision-making, and wasted investment—not because they lack the skills to run a business, but because they underestimate the importance of building a strong internal foundation.

At its core, every business begins inside its builder.

The vision, energy, and resilience of the entrepreneur shaped the trajectory of the business. When the internal foundation is neglected, the external efforts—no matter how strategic—often falter. Emotional and financial lows are part of the entrepreneurial process, but they don't have to derail you. Here's how to build yourself up to sustain your business.

The Wasted Investment: When the Builder is Overlooked

Many entrepreneurs pour countless hours and dollars into their businesses—branding, marketing, inventory, software—without addressing the most critical component of success: themselves. This oversight can lead to wasted resources when burnout or poor emotional health causes:

- **Impulsive Decisions:** Stress clouds judgment, leading to reactive choices rather than strategic planning.
- **Inconsistent Effort:** Emotional fatigue often results in periods of overwork followed by withdrawal, creating instability in the business.
- **Missed Opportunities:** When mental health isn't prioritized, focus diminishes, causing entrepreneurs to overlook growth opportunities or client needs.

Example: A business owner invests $10,000 in a marketing campaign but fails to engage with leads because they're overwhelmed with other responsibilities. Without a solid internal foundation, the return on external investments diminishes.

Strategies to Build Internal Resilience
Set Realistic Expectations

Understanding that growth takes time is one of the most important ways to protect your emotional and financial investment. Overnight success stories are rare and often misleading.

The Reality: Most businesses require 2-3 years to achieve consistent profitability, and the first year is often a period of experimentation and adjustment.

How to Apply: Break long-term goals into smaller, manageable milestones. Celebrate incremental progress—landing your first client, breaking even for the first month, or reaching a new audience.

By aligning expectations with reality, you reduce frustration and build patience for the journey.

Build a Support Network

No entrepreneur succeeds alone. Isolation is one of the leading causes of burnout, as business owners carry the weight of decisions and challenges without external perspective or encouragement.

Joining business owner groups or mentorship programs allows you to share experiences, learn from others' mistakes, and gain encouragement during tough times.

Maintain a professional boundary in most relationships to ensure your business is taken seriously. When connections become overly personal, they can blur the lines and lead to challenges, such as being undervalued or taken advantage of. Be strategic when joining professional groups, as some can be costly with minimal return on investment. However, finding the right group tailored to your business needs can provide significant value and long-term benefits.

Talking to others in the same position normalizes the challenges of entrepreneurship and offers practical solutions.

Example: A solopreneur struggling to manage finances might learn from a colleague about free or low-cost tools, saving themselves hours of stress and potential financial mismanagement.

Prioritize Mental Health

The mental and emotional health of a business owner directly impacts the health of the business. Neglecting self-care leads to diminished focus, creativity, and stamina—critical components for long-term success.

The mental and emotional health of a business owner is the foundation upon which the success of the business rests. Financial deficits and the lack of capital can weigh heavily on an owner's mind, creating constant stress, self-doubt, and anxiety. These hardships often lead to sleepless nights, decision fatigue, and a sense of failure that can erode confidence and derail progress. When self-care is neglected in these moments, focus, creativity, and stamina—the very qualities needed for problem-solving and long-term growth— will begin to diminish.

The pressure of juggling bills, maintaining operations, and trying to grow a business without adequate resources can feel suffocating. It's easy to fall into a cycle of overworking while neglecting physical and emotional well-being. Many business owners internalize their financial struggles, blaming themselves for deficits and viewing their circumstances as personal failures rather than challenges to overcome. This internalization not only impacts the owner but spills over into their relationships, decision-making, and the overall health of the business. Some business owners result in blaming consumers for not choosing their products or services.

To navigate these challenges, it's essential to embrace supportive methods that prioritize mental health while addressing the financial strain. Practicing mindfulness and daily reflection can provide clarity and help separate the business's issues from personal worth. Seeking mentorship or joining a support group of fellow entrepreneurs can provide encouragement, perspective, and practical advice. Leveraging affordable tools to automate and streamline tasks can alleviate some of the operational burden, creating space to focus on what matters most.

It's also important to acknowledge the reality of the situation without shame. Financial deficits and lack of capital are common challenges, not failures. Breaking down financial goals into manageable steps can make them feel less overwhelming while celebrating small wins along the way can restore a sense of progress and accomplishment. If resources allow, consulting a financial advisor to create a realistic plan can ease the mental strain of navigating complex financial waters alone.

At the heart of all this is the understanding that a business owner's well-being is just as vital as the business itself. Investing in mental health is not a distraction from business goals—it's a strategy for achieving them.

By addressing the hardships of financial strain with intentional self-care and supportive practices, business owners can reclaim their strength, resilience, and vision, ensuring both they and their businesses are positioned to thrive.

How to Strengthen Mental Health:
- **Regular Exercise:** Physical activity reduces stress, improves mood, and increases energy levels. Even a 30-minute walk can clear your mind and reset your focus.
- **Mindfulness Practices:** Meditation, journaling, or deep breathing exercises help center your thoughts and manage anxiety.
- **Intentional Rest:** Schedule time for hobbies, family, and

relaxation. These moments of joy and connection recharge your motivation and creativity.

Example: An entrepreneur who blocks time weekly for a favorite activity—whether it's painting, gardening, or spending time with loved ones—often finds they return to their business with renewed energy and perspective.

The Internal Investment That Pays Dividends

Building the internal strength of the entrepreneur isn't just about surviving tough times—it's about thriving through them. When you prioritize your well-being and emotional health, you create a ripple effect:

- **Better Decision-Making:** A clear and focused mind leads to strategic, thoughtful choices.
- **Consistency and Stability:** Clients, collaborators, and employees are drawn to leaders who exude calm, confidence, and vision.
- **Stronger Relationships:** Clients, collaborators, and employees are drawn to leaders who exude calm, confidence, and vision.

Statistical Insight: Entrepreneurs who practice mindfulness and prioritize mental health report 30% higher productivity and a 35% reduction in stress levels (Harvard Business Review).

Reframing Emotional and Financial Lows

It's natural to view setbacks as failures but reframing them as part of the process can change how you approach challenges. For example:

- **Financial Lows:** Instead of focusing on the loss, view it as feedback. What can you learn? How can you adjust?
- **Emotional Lows:** Recognize that these moments are temporary. Implement routines that help you regain perspective.

Example: An entrepreneur who loses a major client may initially feel defeated. By stepping back and analyzing why the client left, they can refine their offerings, improve their processes, and prevent similar losses in the future.

Final Thoughts

The foundation of every successful business lies in the strength, clarity, and resilience of its builder. By setting realistic expectations, cultivating a support network, and prioritizing mental health, you invest in yourself—and by extension, your business. This internal investment ensures that you can weather emotional and financial lows, adapt to challenges, and emerge stronger on the other side.

Remember: Building a business is not just about creating something external—it's about growing the person behind it. When you grow yourself, your business will naturally follow.

Chapter 5
Marketing for Growth: Strategies for Every Stage

Early Phase: Focus on visibility and trust.
- Offer free consultations or samples to attract customers.
- Use local SEO to rank higher in searches for your area.

Growth Phase: Scale with targeted ads and partnerships.
- Run campaigns that highlight your unique selling proposition (USP).
- Collaborate with complementary businesses.

Mature Phase: Build loyalty and refine your brand.
- Launch customer rewards programs.

- Conduct surveys to adapt to customer needs.

Early Stages: Building Visibility and Trust

When your business is just starting, visibility and trust are paramount. At this stage, you're introducing your brand to potential customers and establishing your reputation.

Offer Free Consultations or Samples

Why It Works: Giving people a low-risk way to experience your offerings creates trust and opens the door for long-term relationships. According to Nielsen, 92% of consumers trust recommendations and experiences over advertising.

How to Apply: If you're a service provider, offer a free 15-minute consultation or trial service. Product-based businesses can provide free samples at events or as part of a promotion. This approach allows you to showcase your expertise and build credibility.

Leverage Local SEO

Why It Works: Local SEO ensures your business is easily found by people searching in your area. Studies show that 46% of all Google searches are seeking local information, making this a critical strategy for small businesses.

How to Apply:

Claim your Google My Business profile and optimize it with accurate information, photos, and reviews.

Use location-specific keywords in your website and social media content.

Encourage satisfied customers to leave positive reviews, as these significantly impact local search rankings.

Create Authentic Content
Why It Works: People connect with stories and authenticity. Sharing your journey, challenges, and wins builds a loyal audience.

How to Apply: Use social media to document your business's early days. Post behind-the-scenes photos, customer testimonials, and tips relevant to your industry.

Growth Phase: Scaling with Precision
As your business gains traction, your marketing efforts should focus on scaling strategically. The goal is to expand your reach, refine your brand message, and solidify your position in the market.

Run Campaigns Highlighting Your Unique Selling Proposition (USP)

How to Apply:
- Identify what sets your business apart. What is your superpower as a business owner? (e.g., superior customer

service, eco-friendly products, innovative design). What makes your business truly unique in the marketplace? What is the one "superpower" you bring as a business owner that no one else can replicate? Reflecting on these questions will help you focus on your niche and highlight the strengths that set your business apart from the competition.

- Run targeted digital ad campaigns on platforms like Facebook, Instagram, or Google Ads to highlight this USP.

- Use data analytics to measure campaign performance and refine your approach.

Collaborate with Complementary Businesses

Why It Works: Partnerships allow you to tap into another business's customer base while adding value to your own. It's a cost-effective way to expand your reach.

How to Apply:
- Identify businesses that serve a similar audience but aren't direct competitors (e.g., a home improvement company collaborating with a local real estate agent).
- Create joint promotions or events that benefit both parties.
- Use email marketing or co-branded social media campaigns to promote these collaborations.

Retarget Your Audience

Why It Works: Studies show that retargeting ads can increase conversion rates by up to 150%. These ads re-engage visitors who have shown interest in your business but didn't take action.

How to Apply:

- Use tools like Facebook Pixel or Google Ads to track website visitors.
- Run retargeting ads offering incentives, such as discounts or free resources, to entice these users to return and convert.

Mature Stage: Building Loyalty and Refining Your Brand

In the maturity phase, your business likely has an established customer base. Marketing at this stage focuses on retaining customers, increasing their lifetime value, and ensuring your brand remains relevant.

Launch Customer Rewards Programs

Why It Works: Retaining an existing customer is 5-7 times more cost-effective than acquiring a new one. Rewards programs incentivize repeat business and foster loyalty.

How to Apply:

i. Develop a loyalty program that offers points for purchases, referrals, or social media engagement.

ii. Use a CRM system to track customer activity and

reward milestones (e.g., birthdays, anniversaries with your business).

iii. Promote the program through email marketing and social media.

Conduct Surveys to Adapt to Customer Needs

Why It Works: Listening to your customers ensures you're meeting their evolving needs. Businesses that adapt based on customer feedback are more likely to retain their audience.

How to Apply:

i. Use tools like SurveyMonkey or Google Forms to create customer surveys.

ii. Ask targeted questions about their preferences, pain points, and suggestions.

iii. Implement changes based on their feedback and communicate how their input shaped your decisions.

Enhance Your Brand's Emotional Connection

Why It Works: Emotional connections drive loyalty. Customers who feel connected to a brand have a 306% higher lifetime value (Motista). Motista. (n.d.). **Emotional Connections Drive Loyalty: Customers With Emotional Brand Connections Have 306% Higher Lifetime Value.** *Retrieved from https://www.motista.com*

How to Apply:

i. Share stories that resonate with your audience's values

and aspirations.

ii. Use social proof, like testimonials and case studies, to reinforce the positive impact your business has on its customers.

iii. Engage with your community by sponsoring events, supporting causes, or hosting webinars that align with your brand identity.

A Loss from Neglecting Early Phase Visibility and Trust

In the early phase of my business, I made the critical mistake of not prioritizing visibility and trust. I believed that simply having a good product or service would naturally draw customers, but I underestimated the importance of actively putting my business in front of people and building their confidence in what I offered.

I avoided networking, thinking my personality wasn't suited for it, and relied heavily on passive methods like social media posts without engaging my audience or leveraging relationships. I didn't take the time to create a functional website or focus on professional branding that could build trust and credibility. Instead, I chased quick wins, spending money on flashy marketing tactics that didn't align with my long-term goals.

This neglect cost me valuable time, relationships, and opportunities to establish myself in the marketplace. Potential clients didn't know how to find me or why they should trust my business. In hindsight, I realized how much revenue and growth I missed by not focusing on the foundational elements of visibility and trust early on.

The lesson was clear: if people don't know about your business or feel confident in what you offer, even the best product or service will struggle to succeed. Visibility and trust are not optional; they are the cornerstones of a thriving business.

Final Thoughts: The Long-Term View

Marketing is a dynamic and ever-evolving process that requires continuous adaptation to changes in customer behavior, market trends, and technology. For business owners, the strategies that worked yesterday may not work tomorrow. To remain competitive, you must regularly stay informed, experiment with new methods, and refine your approach.

For example, if social media algorithms shift or customer preferences change, a static marketing plan will fail to resonate. Instead, by treating marketing as an ongoing effort, you can adjust campaigns, leverage data insights, and explore emerging platforms to ensure your message stays relevant and impactful. Flexibility and innovation are key to long-term marketing success.

It evolves alongside your business. As you progress through these stages, remember that successful marketing is customer-focused. Listen to your audience, adapt your strategies, and invest in building trust and loyalty. By doing so, you'll ensure your business not only grows but also thrives in the long run.

Final Words of Encouragement with Prayer

To every business owner starting out or rediscovering their passion, remember this: your vision has value, and your journey matters. The road ahead may feel overwhelming at times, but every great business starts with a single step and the courage to keep moving forward, even when the path isn't clear. Challenges will come, but they are not roadblocks—they are opportunities to learn, grow, and refine your purpose.

It's okay to start small, to pivot, or to take time to rediscover what fuels you. Success is not about perfection; it's about persistence. Celebrate every small win, and don't let setbacks define you. You are capable, resilient, and creative. Trust in your unique gifts and the impact your business can make, no matter how modest the beginnings.

Surround yourself with people who believe in you and seek wisdom from those who have walked similar paths. Remember that no one succeeds alone, and it's okay to ask for help. Stay true to your vision, focus on progress over perfection, and invest in yourself as much as you do in your business.

You were made for this. The work you're doing has the potential to touch lives, change communities, and leave a lasting legacy. Keep going—you're building something extraordinary, one step at a time.

Heavenly Father,

Thank You for the gift of vision and purpose You have placed in every business owner reading this. Your Word says, "Commit to the Lord whatever you do, and He will establish your plans" (Proverbs 16:3). We bring our businesses before You, asking for guidance, wisdom, and strength to persevere through challenges. Let Your favor open doors that no one can shut and provide resources, partnerships, and opportunities that align with Your will.

When discouragement arises, remind us that Your plans are to prosper us, not to harm us, to give us hope and a future (Jeremiah 29:11). Grant us creativity and clarity to make decisions that honor You. Help us to trust in Your timing and to walk in faith, knowing that with You, all things are possible.

Bless the work of our hands, Lord, and let our businesses glorify You and serve others in meaningful ways. In Jesus' name, we pray.

Amen. Thank You!

Dear Reader,

Thank you for investing your time and trust in Win From My Losses. I'm deeply honored to be a part of your journey as you build and grow your vision. Your commitment to learning and growth inspires me, and I hope the insights in this book provide the guidance and encouragement you need.

If you'd like personalized support or strategic advice tailored to your unique journey, I'd love to connect with you. You can book a free or paid consultation with me at www. strategicconnection.me. Together, we can create a roadmap to help you overcome challenges, stay resilient, and achieve your goals.

Thank you again for allowing me to be part of your story. I look forward to supporting you further!
With an unwavering belief in your potential,

Kelle K. Daniels, CEO and Visionary of Strategic Connection L.L.C.
Author of Win From My Losses

About Kelle K. Daniels

Mother, Daughter, Sister, Grandmother, Executive Pastor, Entrepreneur, and Author.

Kelle K. Daniels is a multifaceted leader dedicated to making a positive impact in ministry, business, and community service. With over twenty years of experience in corporate environments, she has excelled in driving innovation, overcoming challenges, fostering growth, and executing strategic initiatives. Her extensive background in entrepreneurship and intrapreneurship equips her to navigate complexities and achieve goals across various sectors.

Kelle is the owner and founder of Strategic Connection L.L.C. Legally established in 2020; the business began practicing in 2010.

Strategic Connection L.L.C. is a premier business consultancy dedicated to empowering high-level business owners in today's fast-paced marketplace. We specialize in providing exclusive, personalized consultation services that help businesses thrive and reach new heights. By crafting robust roadmaps for temporary, short, and long-term success through strategic planning, optimizing operations with dedicated assistance, empowering teams to excel with specialized training, challenging visionaries to expand beyond their comfort zone, and developing effective strategies to handle unforeseen challenges in crisis management.

We ensure your business achieves its full potential. With our proven track record, customized solutions, and comprehensive support, we partner with you to elevate your business strategy and navigate the unique challenges you face.

As an entrepreneur, Kelle has successfully assisted visionaries by developing effective strategies that align vision with tangible outcomes. She specializes in revitalizing existing goals and turning potential debts into profitable ventures. Her expertise in business strategy, financial analysis, marketing solutions, and operational efficiency has empowered those who trust her voice to reach new heights. Kelle's commitment to excellence and her ability to create tailored action plans make her a valuable consultant and strategist.

In her role as Executive Pastor, Kelle brings a deep commitment to spiritual leadership and community development. Her responsibilities extend beyond traditional pastoral duties to include leadership support, organizational development, and fostering a compelling sense of purpose and belonging among her congregation and team. She seamlessly integrates her business acumen with her ministerial calling, enhancing the effectiveness of the organizations she leads.

Driven by her faith, self-confidence, and passion for others, Kelle has pursued extensive training as a Peer Support Specialist and Community Health Worker with the State of Florida, she's also a Support Group Facilitator and Leader with NAMI Emerald Coast, and a Certified Minister of Health through Wesley Theological Seminary. These roles enable her to provide invaluable assistance to help bring awareness to mental health and access vital healthcare resources that support individuals which in turn impacts their families, businesses, and more. Her approach integrates faith with practical support, creating an encouraging environment where individuals can thrive.

Outside of her professional roles, Kelle embraces her blessings as a mother, daughter, and grandmother, finding fulfillment in the relationships she cherishes. She hopes to pass down influential values of courage, resilience, gratitude, and service to future generations in her family.

With a heart for empowerment and dedication to service, Kelle continues to make a meaningful difference in the lives of others. Her combined experience in ministry and business uniquely qualifies her to author works that inspire transformation and growth. By embodying the principles of her faith, purpose, passion, and innovation in all her endeavors, she catalyzes positive change.

"Joyful is the person who finds wisdom, the one who gains understanding."

To find out more information about Kelle K. Daniels, contact for consultation or obtain more powerful hand outs, please refer to the QR Codes below.

Website   Courses/Schedule

Made in the USA
Columbia, SC
03 February 2025

52567081R00035